For The Reckless Sleeper

Amy England

American Letters & Commentary, Inc.

For The Reckless Sleeper

Amy England

For The Reckless Sleeper
Copyright © 2011 by Amy England

All Rights Reserved.

ISBN-10: 0982564716
ISBN-13: 978-0-9825647-1-4

Published by
American Letters & Commentary, Inc.
PO Box # 830365
San Antonio, TX 78283

www.amletters.org

American Letters & Commentary, Inc., is a not-for-profit corporation under section 501(c)(3) of the United States Internal Revenue Code. For over twenty years, AL&C has been dedicated to publishing innovative and "difficult" writing. We are immensely grateful to both the English Department and to The College of Liberal and Fine Arts at The University of Texas at San Antonio for their generous support of our journal. The views expressed in this book, however, are not necessarily those of UTSA, its administration, its employees, or its students, nor are they necessarily the views of AL&C's editors, its volunteers, or its donors.

This is a work of fiction. Any similarities to real people or events are unintentional and are for purposes of illustration.

Front Cover Image: *I See France* © Amy England
Back Cover Image: *I See France2* © Amy England
Cover/Book Design: Catherine Kasper & David Ray Vance

for Eliza, Gabey, Owain, Thomas, Katya and Matthew,

and thank you again, Comrade Apocalypse

For The Reckless Sleeper

Introduction	8
Threat Level Key	9
Doors Closing	11
The Water Tiger	12
Jellyfish Hand	15
Be Careful Of The Snake Pods	16
Gothic Marxism	18
Mice Are At The Curtains	20
Lucy's New Pet	21
Grandaddy Long-Legs	22
Wake Up And Realize That We Must Use The Pit Ponies	23
The Soul Water Must Not Be Spilled	24
I See France	26
My Father's Watch	27
The One-Eyed Man	29
Bus Stop	30
Swimming Parrots	32
The Aquatic Cowboy	34
Beautiful Pigeon	35
Ossuary Cassowary	36
State Park Guide	38
Lumpy Ridge	39

The Mulberry Dragon	46
Grab Up The Human Young And Flee, For The Polar Bear Is Coming To Maul Us All	48
Bombing Map	49
I Do Not Care For Rich People	50
There Is Safety In Being The Eel Man's Grandchild	55
Hotel Midnight	58
A Paladin Stadium In Palladian Arcadia	61
Magic Rice	62
The Disgruntled Tourist	64
Speak No French	68
The Bricks Are Behaving Strangely	70
My Son Has Magic Powers	71
This Is Not Your House	72
Edenic Abundance	73
Applying For Funds	74
Return To Tokyo	76
The Fukushima Nuclear Disaster	77
Whale In The Air	80
Sewing In The Dark	82
Chrome World	84
These Are Elastic Snakes	90
Acknowledgements	91

Introduction

First I had these dreams, and then I wrote them down. Then I rewrote them according to several guidelines. I could use insights into the dream gained after waking, but otherwise, I could only pare down, not add. If I used language that deviated from that dictated by the dream, I moved toward simplicity rather than embellishment. To build up images of the dreams, I started with photographing or finding pictures of the elements that already existed, and made what did not, within the limitations imposed by my rudimentary art skills. Most of the time, while the dreams occur in present tense, events outside them occur in the past.

Working with this material has not led me to refine any particular theory about the relationship between inner and outer worlds, or what dreams mean. I do often get the uncanny feeling that someone else is in there directing my dreams, someone trickier than I am and with a better sense of humor.

— Amy England

Threat Level Key

- Death
- Crushing
- Mauling
- Drowning
- Beaching
- Toxicity
- Getting shot
- Imprisonment
- Loss of valuables
- Discord
- Irritation
- Pinches to fingers and/or toes
- Cold
- Damp

- Scarcity
- Confusion
- Obfuscation
- Nagging unease
- Enthrallment
- Callousness
- Everything solid melting into air
- Monstrous creation
- Unwilling transport
- Inadvertent exhibitionism
- Mystery
- Loss of mystery
- Losing track of time
- Benign

● **Doors Closing**

The Water Tiger ●

New Year festivities in Chinatown. We ate a lot of dim sum and cheered on the parade, the long dragon and tiger puppets. I don't believe in astrology, so I'm a little embarassed at how pleased I am to be born in the year of the tiger, the water tiger to be exact.

That night, I dream of a water tiger. The size of a large house cat, it is swimming in a stream and hunting minnows (my dreams making fun of me—if I am a water tiger, this is the scale we are talking about). The streambed is covered with anenomes and crayfish.

The stream runs outside my uncle's house, and I am about to tell him that he lives near a source of delicious crayfish, but I recall the stream also borders a golf course, and the runoff of pesticides must be terrible.

Uncle Jon, DON'T EAT THE CRAYFISH, I say to him as he gets on the hotel elevator.

He has no idea what I am talking about.

Jellyfish Hand

Be Careful Of The Snake Pods ●

Walking through the jungle, and the guide points out the green pods in which snakes are incubating. "You want to be careful of those."

They look like giant cactus pears, bigger at one end than the other. Some are about the size of a sack of potatoes, and those we lift up grunting and set aside off the path. Some are so large we can't avoid walking on them; in fact the whole jungle floor seems to consist entirely of snake pods.

"You want to be careful of those," the guide says. Although the snakes are dormant, they can still feel the pain of being trampled on, and they don't like it.

I begin to walk more lightly, noticing how the pods feel like cool skin under my bare feet.

I am in a movie theater, the movie about to start. A small pod is wedged into a crevice beside the screen. "You want to be careful of those," I say. And just then a snake does emerge, nematode-like, trailing goo, from a crack in the skin. It is bright green, it trails off, we leave it alone.

Gothic Marxism ●●

I spent an afternoon trying to figure out what kinds of activity my retirement fund was being invested in. That night I had The Dream Of The Vine People:

We have guests, a man and woman dressed in black and white. They are strangely inert, but they *are* our guests, and I try to be hospitable, talking to them as if they are answering me, taking them where they might want to go. The guests each host a horrible parasite, and without them intending it or even noticing, fibrous vines grow out of their sides and into the bodies around them, siphoning off extra nourishment. I know this, and yet somehow I cannot care. They don't mean to. One has to be polite. It will be fine.

The man is standing at the kitchen counter, not noticing that his vines have grown into the chest of our dog. I break the vines, but when I try to pull them out, the dog whimpers in pain. He will be fine. I put him outside.

Soon the neighbors are knocking at the door, the dog in their arms. What kind of monster am I? The dog needs to be put down; his heart is punctured and he is in agony. How could I just put him out and leave him? Blankly I look at them, then shut the door. He will be fine. I take our guests out to breakfast, politely dodging the vines when they grow toward me, ignoring and ignoring that eventually I won't see them coming.

Mice Are At The Curtains

Green net curtains draped over furniture. Gnawing sounds: a mouse is under there somewhere nibbling on the hem. Start pulling up the cloth, thinking to scare the mouse off, yard after yard bunched up in my arms, but the sound continues. Another handful, and suddenly I feel it in my palm, twitching like a castrated thumb. Snap the cloth and fling the thing away. It thumps against the wall. Don't look.

● **Lucy's New Pet**

My sister has a new pet rattlesnake. Mostly it sleeps coiled beside the stairs, where anyone might accidently lay a hand on it. I ask her, isn't it dangerous, and she says yes at first, but eventually you get used to it being there, and learn to be careful.

Grandaddy Long-Legs

As my grandfather sits reading the paper in his chair, a daddy long-legs is crawling about the floor. It is the size of a rat, and its legs are bronze and jointed like some kind of robotic hermit crab. My grandfather would always bat them off the screen door for us, and tell us not to be afraid of them, so I try not to think about this one. But every few minutes, with a start, I notice the scuttling sound it makes. I really am afraid it will bite me. Finally I start making siren noises to scare it away.

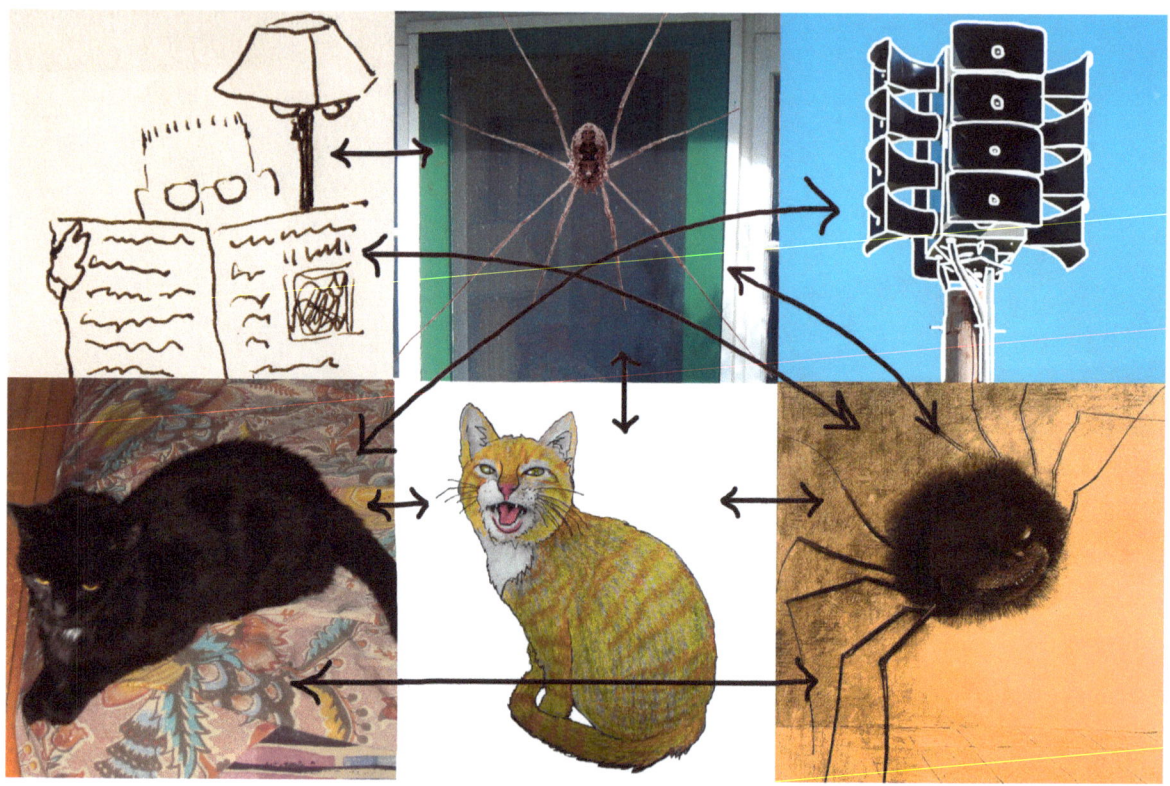

The cats are in a panic over the spider. The black one starts yowling along with my siren, and when I reach down to pet the yellow one, it clamps its little teeth on the very tip of my finger and won't let go, just as I was afraid the spider would do.

Danger/Safety! Everything Is Everything Else!

● Wake Up And Realize That We Must Use The Pit Ponies

Student party at a large messy house in Cambridge, Massachusetts. While not stylish, the house has a certain Art Deco charm in its black and white decorated door frames. The party is also a front for our plan to smuggle out a large bag of red lentils preserved in oil. Now word has arrived that the government is on to us, and soldiers are surrounding the house, and you, our leader, have fainted dead away.

Patiently, I am waiting for you to come to and realize the inevitable. We must negotiate the release of our pit ponies (all will agree that these innocent blind creatures should not be caught in the conflict). Then we will drape a blanket over their backs, and you and I will crouch between them (holding, of course, the *bag of lentils*) and slip out of the house. Yes, eventually we will be spotted, but by then we'll be far enough away to escape. I've seen this movie before.

The Soul Water Must Not Be Spilled 🟡⚫

The thrilling part of Wolf Cave is the stretch at the end, so tight and black and twisted that it doesn't seem you will ever come out, just as the passage squeezes you through a small hole into daylight on the other side of the hill. I went through it once about ten years ago, some small boys ahead of me and their father behind, and even with their voices around me it was disconcerting.

This past winter, we were hiking in the empty park, and I started through the cave again. It's really a very short distance. But as the light disappeared, and water began to cover the floor, and I had to drop to my hands and knees to crawl below an overhang, I lost my enthusiasm. The smell of wet clay. Why would I go down there voluntarily? It was like wanting to die. I stumbled back out the way I came, ashamed of myself.

Next morning we found that Kali, our rickety and fiercely unfriendly cat, had had a stroke. She couldn't walk or pick up her head. She hadn't eaten or drunk anything, and she'd peed on the floor. When we put her in the car, she pedaled her legs, pushing her head into any corner she could find, trying to get to the dark.

A little water in a steel chalice. The bowl of the chalice is nested in a complex of rings, like a gyro-compass, so that however you tilt it, the water will not spill out. When I pick up the chalice, I hear it crying with the voice of our dead cat. I wrap it in the gray flannel that I use to cushion my violin in its case, and hold the bundle to my shoulder. Little phalanges of steel begin kneading me just as she used to do.

I See France ●

I want to see a city, I say to myself as I fall asleep. And I do dream that my husband and I are looking down from our hotel window in Paris onto ornately decorated doorways and labyrinthine alleyways. But then we get distracted by the risque fact that we are in a hotel room. No need to close the curtains; up so high, who will notice us?

At an embarassing moment, I see that the rooftops of Paris are crowded with construction workers or maybe firemen, all making catcalls and cheering. I, subject, want to see, verb, a city, object, not the other way round, but my dreams do not care about syntax. Or perhaps they are making fun of me again. We know what you really want.

●● My Father's Watch

It is hard, at first, to read my father's watch.

But if you put your eye to it, as to the eyepiece of a telescope, you will see...

all the modes of time.

"I shall never forget that luminous journey on that brightest of winter nights. The colored map of the heavens expanded into an immense dome, on which there loomed fantastic lands, oceans and seas, marked with the lines of stellar currents and eddies, with the brilliant streaks of heavenly geography... The moon still rode high in the sky. The transformations of the sky, the metamorphoses of multiple domes into more and more complicated configurations were endless. Like a silver astrolabe, the sky disclosed on that magic night its internal mechanism and showed in infinite evolutions the mathematics of its cogs and wheels."
— Bruno Schulz

● The One-Eyed Man

To train yourself in lucid dreaming, begin by trying to dream of looking at your own hands. This is how Richard Feinman said he learned to do it.

We are walking down alleys behind people's houses, and it doesn't look like the restaurant could possibly be here, but I assure my friends it is—a modest, shabby place, but wonderful. We file in—it looks like someone's basement—and sit down on the folding chairs, talking the whole time. In a mirror I see that I have become a one-eyed man. My hair is shaved to stubble, my jaw is almost wider than my face, and the scar over the dead eye is a little hard to look at, but I think with satisfaction that the ladies all seem to like it well enough. I stop talking because I am now too cool to chatter away like some girl. But I am also too cool to sit looking in the mirror, so I sit looking at my hands for a long time.

When I told my husband about this dream, I thought the strange thing was that I had changed genders and lost half my sight and was so pleased about it. He gave me one of those looks he reserves for my worst cases of obliviousness. Later I remembered what "one-eyed man" could be a euphemism for. The bald head. The wide jaw. The arrogant attitude. The fascination with my hands . . .

Bus Stop

Dozens of us crowd into the bus stop. The black screen sides are woven with purple tissue paper graffiti, suggesting a new and delightful way to enliven public space. But this is a fake bus stop, really a net erected by the police, and now they surround us to haul us off. Who thought of the tissue paper? It is an especially nefarious touch.

The first protest in Chicago against the Iraq War, which was entirely peaceful and did no harm worse than disrupting traffic, ended with police cordoning off the crowd and arresting everyone they could, somewhere between six and eight hundred people.

At the next protest, Federal Plaza was surrounded by police buses, and mounted police, and every officer in the area had been called in, dressed in full riot gear, to keep us contained within their ranks at all times, as if we carried a disease and needed to be quarantined. Compared to the risks many take, it was nothing dramatic. But I still feel compelled to describe it, the endless carapaces of helmets and shields and bristlings of clubs and plastic handcuffs. How faceless they became, what weird insects they turned into.

Swimming Parrots

As we stand at the railing looking down at the resort pool, I notice that you are dressed in the splendid satin outfit of a country and western singer, suggesting abilities I did not know you possessed. The parrots plunge in and out of the pool. Could parrots always swim, and I just didn't notice? Can I trust this benign state of affairs to continue?

[The National Council on Dream Safety addresses this rash dream.
Do not be lulled into a fool's paradise; this is not a country and western song.
Parrots cannot swim. Do not take your parrot swimming.]

The Aquatic Cowboy ●

The very rare aquatic cowboy, here shooting it out with his natural enemies, the shore folk.

● Beautiful Pigeon

Avitrol, commonly used to poison pigeons, attacks their nervous system, causing them hours of painful convulsions as they fly around bashing into things until it finally kills them. Often other birds eat the poisoned bait and die as well.

Few species can survive the pollution of the city, but the pigeons on the roof of our apartment building had the nerve to thrive there. We told each other they were causing diseases, although this was not true. It was true that their arrogant cooing woke us up early, and they soiled our fine balcony furniture. We made them pay.

Ossuary Cassowary

Tail feathers trailing like the train of a beaded sea-green evening gown. Small birds camouflage themselves by riding on the corresponding colors on the cassowary's back. The blue one hides its face under its wing.

State Park Guide

1. PARKING LOT: after our hike, we are going to set up our tent in the campground nearby.

2. ENTRANCE TO ICE CAVE: I look around, but already I have lost track of you.

3. RANGER'S STATION: kept as it was a hundred years ago, that is, absolutely empty. People mill around. I check this map and decide to return by the alternate route, assuming you'll catch up eventually.

4. A NAKED WOMAN AND HER MANY CHILDREN CARVED INTO A ROCKY OUTCROP.

5. STATUE OF A GRASSHOPPER: inside it is hollow and filled with napping children. How annoying that people don't look after their children adequately and we have to put up with them sleeping in our state monuments.

And how annoyed you must be with me, love. The hike is nearly over, and I never managed to find you. Perhaps you never left the parking lot, and are still in the car, mildly seething.

● **Lumpy Ridge**

Chicago or Denver now has an elevated pedestrian mall over the street, full of kitchy southwestern souvenirs that it has NOT earned, not being in the southwest… dried chili peppers and fake Hopi pots and beaded necklaces…

… the honeycomb of little booths, slightly dusty… an Escher-like ubiquity of steps, many of which you can't use, fake adobe built in the eighties… already falling apart, ending in air, like so much from the eighties…

Why am I paying attention to this capitalist nonsense? The train platform is right above me. From up there, I should have a superb view of the Rockies.

Yes, there are the Rockies, and over there, where Lake Michigan should be, I look out instead...

. . . on Lumpy Ridge! that astonishing batholithic formation, except now it's in colored layers as if it were also formed *sedimentally*.

Let's sit down and look at it. The most pleasurable, delicate juxtapositions of blue and green and gold and dark red, the layers cutting across arches and pillars . . .

Why am I moving?

Drat. I accidentally sat down in the shopping trolley, and now I'm being whisked away to go shopping against my will.

The Mulberry Dragon

1538, earlier taragon, from Middle French targon, variant of tarc(h)on from Middle Latin tragonia, from Byzantine Greek tarchon, from Arabic tarkhon, from a non-Arabic source, perhaps Greek drakon (from drakontion "dragonwort"). See Indo-European root *derk-*, to see, suffixed zero grade from drk-on(t)-, DRAGON, DRAKE, RANKLE, TARRAGON, Greek drakōn, serpent, dragon (from "monster with the evil eye").

At
night,
when we
were the dragon's
children, we played at
hanging upside down from the
trees around the bonfire he had built
for us, and the shadows we made looked like
bats. Then one of us got frozen to a branch in the
cold, and the dragon had to crawl, carefully and slowly
because he was very old, up to the treetop to get him down. The
boy got free on his own, but the dragon was so cold and exhausted
from his efforts that he turned into a silkworm to rest. We go to visit him. The
silkworms are eating leaves in a little wooden cage. You bump into me and I fall with
a hand on either side of the cage, almost crushing it. The silkworm bodies are pale
green and translucent like unripe mulberries. An old Chinese man is tending
them. As I follow him along a narrow wooden walkway through the
bright trees, I look at him carefully, and see the dragon in his
face, so I know he is trustworthy. Between forefinger and
thumb, he holds a small fruit, bruised on one side
and leaking juice. He says, This should restore
our friend. I can't remember what
it's called, though. Tarragon,
Dagon, I think, and then,
no, it's a miniature
dragon fruit,
I say.

Grab Up The Human Young And Flee, For The Polar Bear Is Coming To Maul Us All

We are wading through the cascades in the basement when we find a polar bear cub. In a flash we realize that its mother is at this moment mauling her way through the city above, for she senses that between her and her cub we are the chief obstacle.

●● Bombing Map

All right, so here, we've set the bomb targets according to this map, this is where we're bombing now. You what? You want to hold the map? I suppose so, the coordinates are set already, I don't see how it could matter. Although actually I'm a bit nervous about this. Could I have the map back please? I know I said it shouldn't matter, but now that I'm not holding the map, the bombs are not landing accurately, I can tell. This is not a thing to do any which way!

No, the bombs don't make any noise. They're the silent kind. In fact, the only way, in the middle of the night like this, that you can tell they've landed, is that you can hear where they hit become more silent. You don't consciously hear the sound of a town far away, but you do hear it, a little vapor of white noise, traffic and electric humming and sirens and so on, and I can tell, from some change in this vapor, that we are not hitting what we meant to. Do you hear that large silence off on the horizon now? That's Cincinnati or something.

I Do Not Care For Rich People 🟢🔵

We are doing our spring cleaning, so the furniture is on the lawn. Our prize possession is a curved antique bench, Arts and Crafts period, inlaid with panels of black slate.

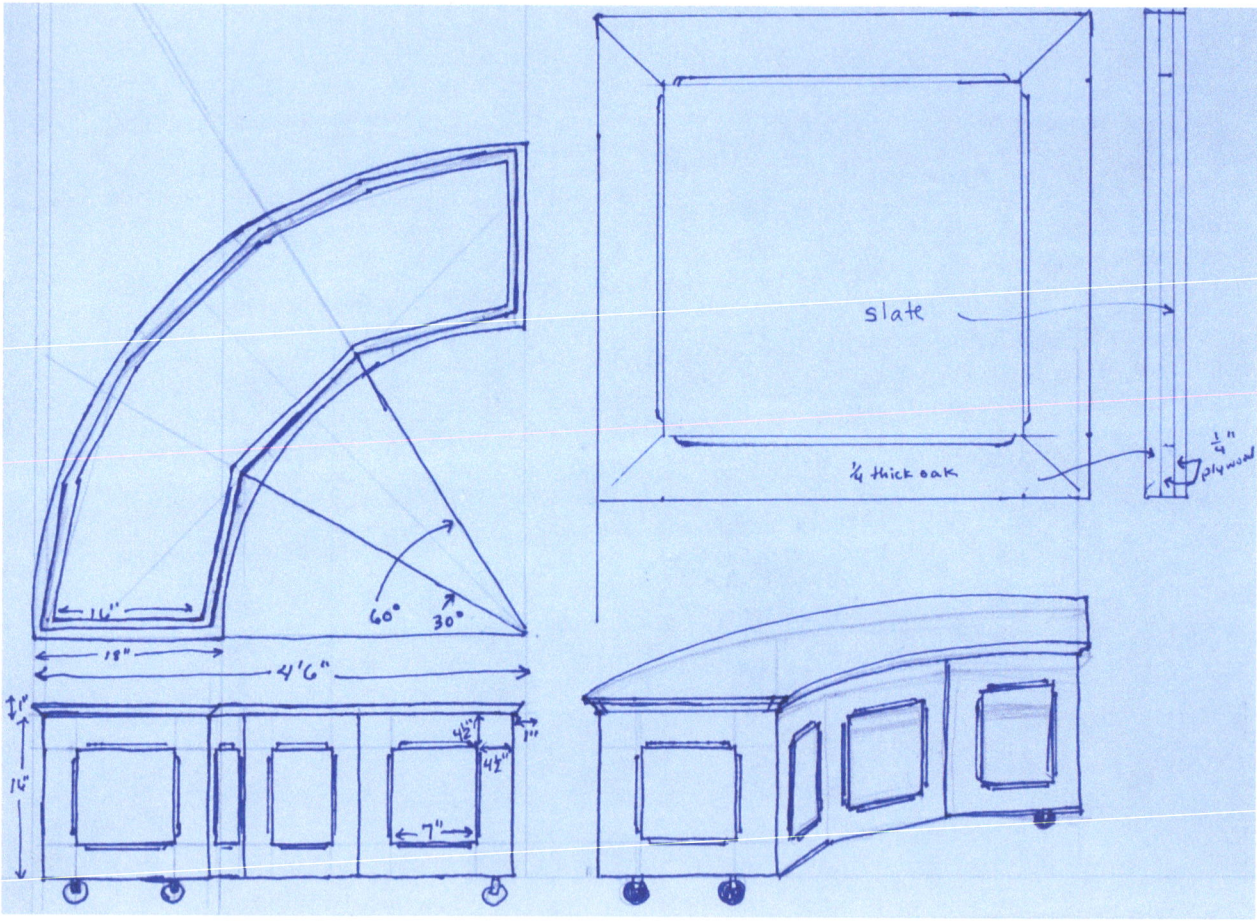

The man who lives in the mansion across the street keeps stealing it, claiming that since we left it out, we must be throwing it away. And now he is at it again, in his pajamas, pushing the bench up his driveway.

GIVE THAT BACK, I yell after him in pure rage.

Pushing the recovered bench along the outside of their high wrought iron fence, I encounter his anime character wife. "Are you blind?" she asks. "Because I can't abide the blind."

More rage. I am pretty sure she is blind herself,

as she demonstrates a moment later when she turns into a borzoi and tries to bite me. I hold out a cardboard box. She bites it, thinks it was my arm, and is satisfied.

The last I see of her, she is dancing on her lawn among the giant chess pieces.

○ There Is Safety In Being The Eel Man's Grandchild

A villain out of an Edwardian melodrama, and a genuine relative of Satan, he also looks very like a Javanese shadow puppet.

When in a hurry, he can turn into a huge black eel and dart through the air, just as he is doing now, rushing to the front doors of his Edwardian men's club, for his grandchildren have arrived.

And indeed here we are.

We spend the afternoon showing Grandfather the games we like, our jacks and mud pies. He is delighted with each one.

Every few minutes we recall that we are deathly afraid of him. But though he might fillet a man alive before our eyes, he would never injure either of us.

Javanese shadow puppets often have flame-shaped embellishments.

The little pots of sterno burn also, blue under the chafing dishes in the Edwardian men's club banquet room.

Hotel Midnight ●●

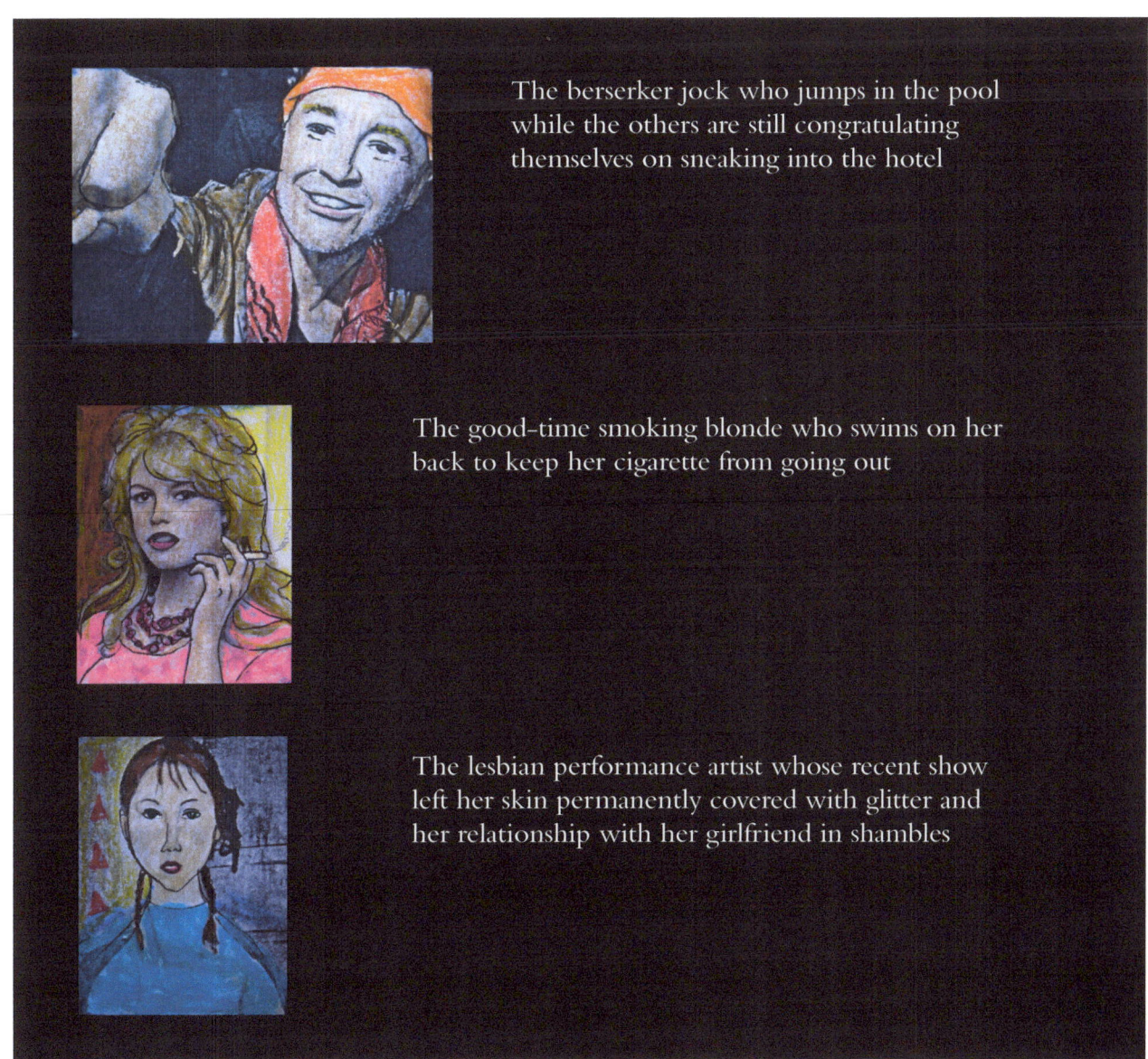

The berserker jock who jumps in the pool while the others are still congratulating themselves on sneaking into the hotel

The good-time smoking blonde who swims on her back to keep her cigarette from going out

The lesbian performance artist whose recent show left her skin permanently covered with glitter and her relationship with her girlfriend in shambles

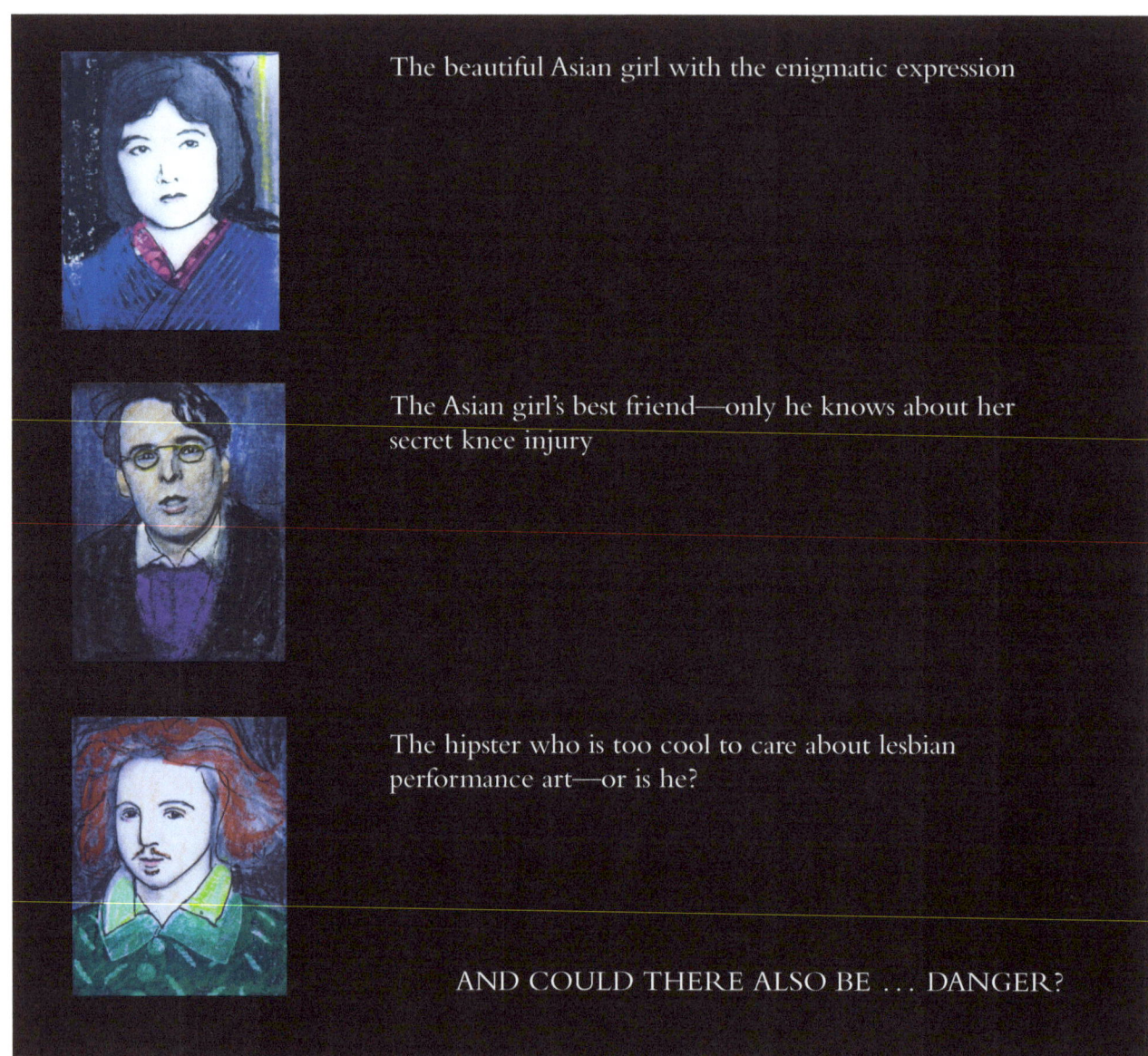

● A Paladin Stadium In Palladian Arcadia

Seeing prophetic meanings in the motion of a rattlesnake, we set up our own fortune telling business, HP Fortunes. The HP stands for Hibernium Palladium. It *takes OFF*. Eventually, we decide to live up to our name and make our headquarters in Ireland, but now we are having problems. "No, you cannot take hundreds of rattlesnakes into Ireland," they are telling us at customs.

Magic Rice ●

I work as a waitress at a restaurant famous for its magic rice. The perk making the job worthwhile is that I get to take the rice home and eat it for every meal, even breakfast.

Unbeknownst to me or anybody, the only person who knows the magic rice recipe is our Filipino dishwasher, a tough guy with a red scooter.

He makes the rice in his superhero persona, the Iron Butterfly.

The Disgruntled Tourist ●

For a thousand years, people in Scandinavia have celebrated the festival of the summer solstice with a parade between two tumuli, one small and round, with a spout of water pouring out the side, and the other larger and rectangular, now covered with trees. But when the disgruntled tourist comes to see the parade, he finds it disgustingly dominated by Sesame Street characters and other American children's TV icons. He could have seen the same thing at home.

Disgruntled, he stomps off into the woods. Families are sitting on the ground having solstice picnics. He thinks of saying hello as he stomps by, then thinks better of it.

Along the flat rocks and mud that edge the many streams, he sees solstice offerings of currency and paper cut up like currency—bills not only from Scandinavia, but all over the world. Any important paper would make a suitable offering, and he thinks of setting down the racing form in his hand. But no, he still needs it. "Out of Shadow Valley," says the racing form, referring to his favorite horse, both its parentage and its geographical origins. Shadow Valley is right around here somewhere, and the racing form conveniently includes directions.

Still, he is surprised when the valley appears suddenly beneath his feet—he almost steps off into the air. The huge crater of an extinct volcano, it has nearly vertical walls and a gentle dome as its floor. Soft green vegetation covers it, and a fine, closely adhering layer of wispy fog. Valley lost to time! Populated by wild horses! He wants to go down there as he has never wanted anything in his life.

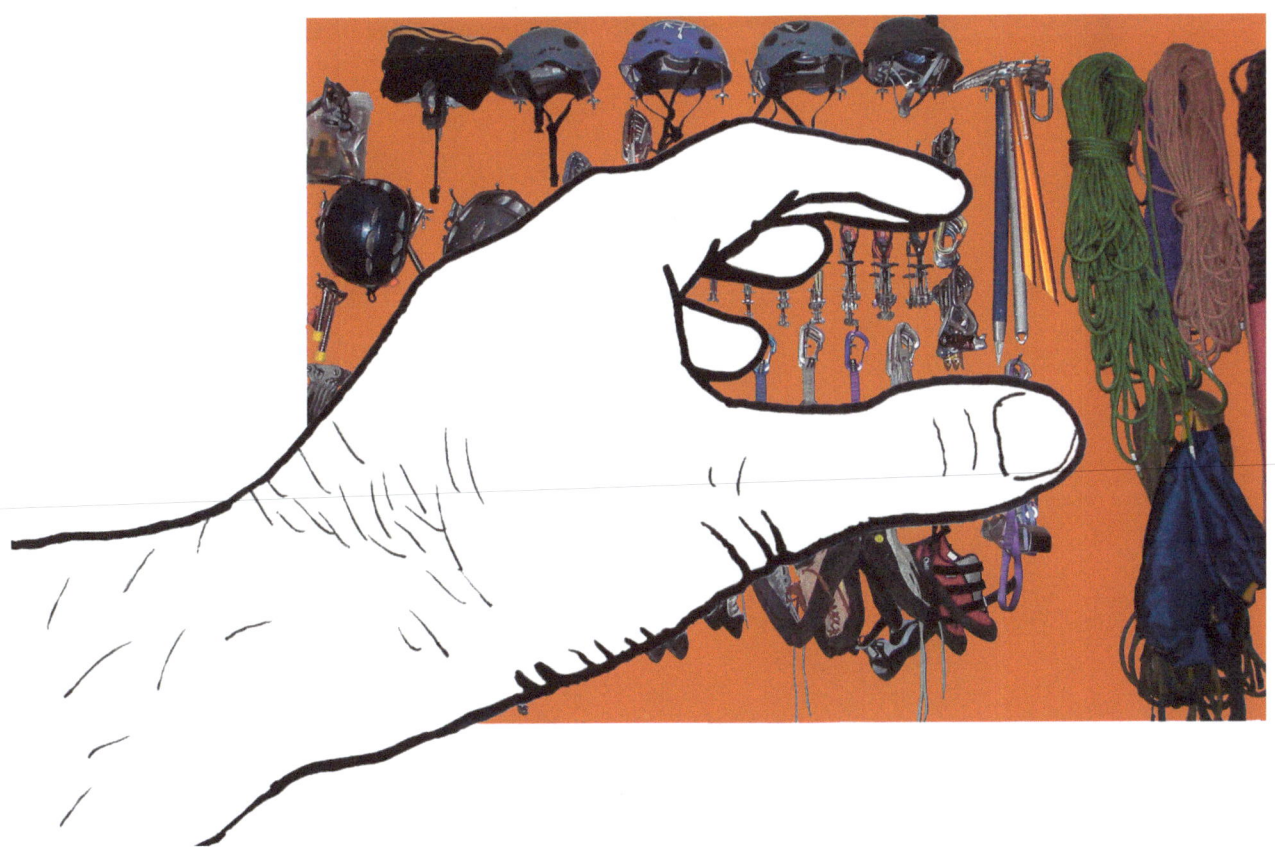

Back in the hotel room, he tells this to his roommates. "Shadow Valley?" says one. "I've done that climb before, but I would love to go back. I'll take you." The room is full of climbing equipment; they can all easily make the trip. The disgruntled tourist is first elated, then depressed. So anyone can go there, really.

Speak No French We Beg Of You ●

An unnameable terror roams the Viking–Inuit ruins. This Québécois tourist ignored the warnings. Now he lies on the tundra, stripped of his parka, stunned and pink with cold.

(In his book on the collapse of civilizations, Jared Diamond describes the medieval Norse settlements in Greenland. Although they shared Greenland with the Inuit, who demonstrated before their eyes how to live successfully within the limits of the Greenland climate, the Norse scarcely acknowledged the existence of these people. Certainly they did not deign to adopt any Inuit strategies for survival, even as they starved to death.)

The Bricks Are Behaving Strangely ●

My Son Has Magic Powers

My teenage son has developed magic powers. For some reason the thing that enrages me most is that he keeps teleporting a girl he likes into the house. I'm telling a friend about this, and she shows me in the mirror that my eyes are glowing yellow-green as if I were a character from a horror movie. So I have magic powers too. "I'll need them," I say; "no one should have to live like this." I pull the girlfriend through the pipes in the wall, locket first, to give her a talking to.

This Is Not Your House ●

Be Vigilant:

● **Edenic Abundance**

Sometimes we see a stray black cat, or maybe a small panther, lurking in our weedy back yard. It is very skittish, and will not let us approach it. To demonstrate my good intentions, I start petting other cats and dogs that have wandered by. Word seems to get out. More dogs and cats crowd up. Finally the stray cat joins us. It is an orgy: I am lying on the grass, petting and petting the soft fur and cold noses of more quivering, enthusiastic bodies than I have hands for.

Applying For Funds

What research facilities do you plan to use in Japan? I'll have to do some research to answer that one. What is the purpose of your proposed visit? I don't even have an answer to that yet.

What am I doing, anyway, I can't just leave my job and everything; this is a waste of time. Just fill in the easy ones and figure out the rest later.

It occurs to me that I haven't seen the frying pan since I finished with it. Where did it go? The place is a mess, as usual, but it was right here . . . where did Bob put it? Always putting my stuff just anywhere, when this was obviously important, anyone could see that . . .

There it is, in with the dirty dishes. Stacked on top of the dirty dishes, even though I made the flowers out of actual rubies.

Return To Tokyo ●

Since last I was here, Tokyo has become even more entirely made of text. I can't read a word of it. Well, I'm not just going to enjoy being confused like I did last time. I want a map, I want a dictionary, I'm not going a step farther until I get them.

●● The Fukushima Nuclear Disaster

In the wake of the tsunami, I fall asleep wondering how Japan is faring in my dreams. And dream I am reading poems at a high school in Wisconsin. I accidentally fall asleep in the classroom, and when I wake up, the teacher is trying to rape me. Leave me the FUCK alone, I scream, and flee down the empty hallways of the dark Gothic nighttime public school in Wisconsin. I wake up, I mean wake up wake up, with wave after wave of horripilation electrifying my arms. Trying to understand things through your dreams is like trying to skewer them with a live snake. Perhaps that public school teacher felt the same way.

Why did I dream this? Given the present attacks on public education workers and what's left of the unions in Wisconsin, teachers there are the rapees, not the rapists, but subject-verb-object syntax is not something my dreams have much regard for, as I said before. Perhaps the dream really is about Japan. Certainly this level of visceral terror is a more suitable response to what is happening there. (After Chernobyl, I always thought that we would have the honor of first proving that democratic capitalism couldn't be trusted with nuclear power, either.) Or perhaps my poor brain simply shortcircuited trying to figure out what to be afraid of.

The next night's dream is more to the point, though it still registers personal threat rather than empathy. I have invited a lot of people to my house, and the more that arrive, the more things go wrong. The sink is leaking; one of my students is mopping up great puddles of rusty water. And now little silver origami creatures are sneaking in under the door.

I stretch a hand down to one, and sure enough, it tries to clamp onto my finger, never to let go. We lift rugs and tatami mats, finding and crushing one silver metal flower after another. As soon as we turn our backs on them, they uncrush themselves and are after us again. I am looking for a glass jar large enough to keep them all. I open the back door and see that more are slinking up the steps.

Whale In The Air ●

There is a *whale* in the *air*. I grab the arms of the friends on either side of me, but they don't believe me and won't look up.

Tiny as a biplane, she is flexing her tail at the peak of her leap.

Now they look, but she has already belly-flopped back into Lake Michigan, although they do see the splash, higher than the trees.

Now she is cavorting in the water, and I am waving to her and shouting. She is spotted brown and white like a dairy cow, because she is a whale cow.

Now she is swimming toward me. I am afraid she will beach herself on the sand and die, that my calling to her, even that slight gesture, will bring her to harm. But this joyful abandon could not possibly end badly.

Sewing In The Dark

I am in the passenger seat of a car driving through the night. I am covered with pieces of slippery fabric that I am sewing, into what I have no idea, but if I fit them together correctly the object will emerge whether I understand what I am doing or not.

We arrive at the theater of our destination. They are setting up the scenery of huge pillow houses and trees.

I strain to see the enormous tentacled thing that I now realize I was sewing together in the car.

Chrome World ●●

I am charged with the care of a wild old man. He's completely irascible, and I can't get him to wear any more than this loin cloth made of dead leaves and packing tape. Here I am trying to herd him into his trailer to go to bed. He and his airstream attract a lot of tame deer that will let you hug them if you want to.

And here is the wild old man at an art colony.

I wonder if I could score a stay at the art colony myself? Because I am in love with the chrome spheres of the studios.

On the esplanade beyond the colony is the conservatory for chrome plants.

It is unclear whether the conservatory was built around the plants, or whether they grew to fit the building's shape.

Beyond that, a row of townhouses displays a retro-futuristic pattern of chrome ornament.

Whatever forms of chrome fill the world beyond that, I can see no farther.

These Are Elastic Snakes: Not Dangerous ○

Acknowledgements

People too numerous to mention have looked at these images and offered suggestions, but I would especially like to thank Dr. Lucinda England, model; Frank Rogaczewski for his proofreading; the Next Objectivists at the Mess Hall for their beautiful exchange of dreams; and the participants in the Durutti Skool reading at the Red Rover Series for their useful discussion on poetry and politics.

Notes

P. 60: Jared Diamond, *Collapse*, Penguin Books, 2011, 261-73 passim.

P. 11: Bruno Schulz, *The Street of Crocodiles and Other Stories*, Penguin Books, 2008, 61-62.

P. 18: Based on a photograph by Jon Gresham (with permission).

P. 70: Based on a photograph by Beverly Stewart (with permission).

About The Author

Amy England has a B.A. from Brandeis University, an M.A. from University of Illinois at Chicago and a Ph.D. from the University of Denver. She is the author of two books of poetry: *The Flute Ship Castricum*, and *Victory and Her Opposites: A Guide* (illustrated by Mary Olson and Karen Andrews). Both books are published by Tupelo Press. She lives in Rogers Park in Chicago and teaches in the creative writing program at the School of the Art Institute.

www.ingramcontent.com/pod-product-compliance
Lightning Source LLC
Chambersburg PA
CBHW042012150426
43195CB00003B/98